Teach Me to Pray

Loyola Press

There were once two children
who wanted to talk to God,
but they did not know how to pray.

The children found their mother
and asked her how to pray.
"I know!" said the mother.
"You have to be very, very quiet."

So they were all very, very quiet.
But nothing happened,
and they could not pray.

The children and their mother
found the children's father
and asked him how to pray.
"I know!" said the father.
"You have to kneel down."

So they all knelt down
and were very, very quiet.
But nothing happened,
and they could not pray.

The children and their mother and their father
found the children's grandpa
and asked him how to pray.
"I know!" said the grandpa.
"You have to put your hands together."

So they all put their hands together,
and they knelt down
and were very, very quiet.
But nothing happened,
and they could not pray.

The children and their mother and their father
and their grandpa found the children's
grandma and asked her how to pray.
"I know!" said the grandma.
"You have to close your eyes."

So they all closed their eyes,
and they put their hands together,
and they knelt down
and were very, very quiet.
But nothing happened,
and they could not pray.

The children and their mother and their father
and their grandpa and their grandma
found the nice lady next door and asked her
how to pray.
"I know!" said the lady.
"You have to go to church."

So they all went to church,
and they closed their eyes,
and they put their hands together,
and they knelt down
and were very, very quiet.
But nothing happened,
and they still could not pray.

The children and their mother and their father
and their grandpa and their grandma
and the nice lady next door
found the pastor and asked him how to pray.
"I know!" said the pastor.
"But it's not what you think."

"Being very, very quiet is splendid,
and kneeling down
and putting your hands together
and closing your eyes
and going to church
are all fine things to do."

"But if you want to talk to God,
you must learn to listen."
"Listen?" said the little girl.
"Just listen?" said the little boy.
"Really listen," said the pastor.

So the children and their mother and their father
and their grandpa and their grandma
and the nice lady next door and the pastor
all listened.
And then they knew God was with them,
and they prayed.

"I can listen to God at church," said the boy.
"Or at home," said the girl.
"When I'm quiet," said their mother.
"Or when I'm loud," said their father.

"When I kneel," said their grandpa.

"Or when I turn cartwheels," said their grandma.

"With my eyes closed," said the pastor.

"Or wide open," said the nice lady next door.

Then they all clapped their hands
and made a lot of noise
and leaped about
and waved their arms around

and sang and danced
and laughed and hugged—
because they had learned how to pray.

"Thank you, God, for teaching us to listen. Now we can pray every day!"

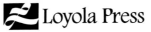
Loyola Press

3441 North Ashland Avenue
Chicago, Illinois 60657

©1999 John Hunt Publishing; Text ©1999 Pennie Kidd
Illustrations ©1999 Toni Goffe

Design by Graham Whiteman

ISBN 0-8294-1368-5

Printed in Hong Kong/China

99 00 01 02 03 / 10 9 8 7 6 5 4 3 2 1